I0483546

The Startup Survival Guide

Jason Criddle

ISBN-13: 978-1515392415
ISBN-10: 1515392414

I write a lot of books – which makes for a lot of dedications and acknowledgements. No matter what I ever write, at the end of the day, all of my credit goes to my beautiful little girl. She awoke the sleeping giant within me… My Schnookums.

THE STARTUP SURVIVAL GUIDE

I have spent so much time writing and delegating over the last year or so, that I almost completely lost sight of just how huge my brand and businesses have become. From the outside it may seem like my life is full of rainbows and jelly beans, but there is a constant gnawing and pulling at my inner being. There are times when I cannot eat, sleep, leave the house, drink water, or conjure up the strength to scratch my nose. There are unanswered questions, never-ending to-do lists, and thousands of unanswered calls and emails tugging at my pant leg every time I take a moment to breathe. This folks, is the life of an entrepreneur. But not just the average entrepreneur—an entrepreneur that is developing a global brand and empire.

The clock says 3AM, and I cannot remember if I woke up early or just haven't been to sleep. All I know is, days of the week no longer matter to me, my legacy does. But I need help... I need an answer. What can I do right now to stay productive? Here is a notepad—that is a good start. Now, what do I write? What if... what if I could come up with a checklist of 5 to 8 questions... hmm – questions? Steps? Things...? Help me out guys, I am not sure how to word it... a list of survival rules for a guy like me...? Not just a guy with a small business, but a guy building a kick ass global empire.

Anyway, as I began making this list, I figured it would make a great chapter to a book, but as the list grew to 12, 15, then 20 items and beyond, I figured it may make a good little publication on its own. Hell, after constantly adding to and updating the content, a couple of years from now, it could very well be a list of 100 principles, with its own hardcover edition. Yes!!

Principles!! That is what I will call them!

So, I give you, "The Startup Survival Guide: An ongoing list of necessary principles for someone building a bad ass global empire." The title may change one day, but for right now, I am standing by this one. ☺

I didn't want to create an extravagant list of any sort, nothing above conventional. Nothing with a "WOW" factor. Nothing over the top. Just some common sense factors I did not take into account when I started building my global empire; covering topics I wish someone had covered with me so I could have saved myself thousands of dollars' worth of mistakes, as well as cherished time I will never get back. Take these principles with a grain of salt. Some of them may resonate with you, some may not. But I can promise you, I really wish I had read these in a book when starting my own entrepreneurial journey.

Welcome to the ever-expanding list of my own personal business principles. I promise to give you a list of 100 someday.

1. Your business will only grow as large as your thinking.

There are so many bumper sticker quotes I can think of right now which would make great analogies for this particular topic, but a very relatable one would be, "Whether you think you can, or think you can't -- you are right."

Or thoughts dominate our reality, and whatever we are striving to reach, we very well can and will reach it if we put forth the effort it will take to reach it. Most of the time, that has a lot less to do with performing physical actions as it does with becoming the person needed to fulfill your ultimate desires. Even if there is drastic action that needs to be taken, trying to take that action without changing you think will just leave you sitting on the curb, throwing rocks, and wondering why another entrepreneurial endeavor failed.

Henry Ford was the man who said the quote I listed above. Ford did not just want to build a tiny car company—he wanted to make the first car that would be affordable to the entire population. He also wanted to build an assembly line that could pop those puppies out around the clock. In the fall of 1908, the first Model T left the production plant with a multi-faceted assembly line that could assemble a brand new Model T in just 24 seconds. Whether he had set out to build 10 cars a year, or hundreds per day, he was right. And you can be too. The time is going to pass anyway. You may as well think HUGE and KICK ASS doing it!

2. If you wouldn't, don't expect them to...

In the beginning stages of running my investment firm back in 2014, I came across a lot of "great" ideas. A ton of inventors with contraptions aimed at changing the planet or the way we wash our socks. I met all sorts of artists who never let anyone else see or hear their work before asking for a million dollars to market it. I saw Power Point presentation after Power Point presentation about gadgets and gizmos of plenty, and who's-its and what's-its galore… and if you wanted thing-a-ma-bobs, they had plenty. And they always wanted more and more money. Countless people would come to us with an idea written on paper, and ask for hundreds of thousands, if not millions, of dollars.

In the early stages of the company, we were trying to get capital for everyone who came to us, but we noticed a trend: an approval rating of less than 5%. Why? Because we never took the time to see if their product, plan, or service held any weight. With no sweat equity, effort, or their own capital thrown into a project, how would they expect anyone else to front them any cash? Sadly, they did. But it pushed me to the point to where I would simply ask my potential clients, "How much have you invested in your project?"

This principle does not just apply to investing either. Ask yourself if you would purchase your product. Ask yourself if you would pay for your service. Look at your value proposition from someone else's perspective, or do your best to get genuine feedback from a test group of people. Whether it has to do with purchasing or investing, if you wouldn't, don't expect them to.

3. Focus on building your name more than any product or service.

After being in network-marketing for quite some time, helping people build their own teams of asset and building my own brands, I have learned a valuable fact: no matter what you have to sell, provide, or hold someone's hand into doing, if you have a name for yourself, your job is done. And you don't build a name for yourself overnight. You must give back to your customers, your community, or all of humanity – it just depends on how large your goals are and what your purpose is on this planet. No one cares about your sales script, they want to know that you give a damn about their needs.

"To-do" lists are not as important as affirmation and manifestation practices, consciously changing habits and making better decisions for your future, or assuring yourself of your worthiness to achieve your desires. You must realize though, achieving those desires depends on who YOU are. People follow people, not products. Who are you? How do people see you? Do you wow people enough to desire an association with you, or do you push people away with your negative outlook on life; or forceful sales tactics? People should expect nothing out of you except greatness. You should be known for your ambition, honesty, drive, creativity, and everything you have done to actively progress the planet.

4. Relationships will make or break you.

I have had just as many business partners steal from me and stab me in the back as I have had intimate partners from former relationships. While luckily that number is very few, it still sucks when someone makes conscious decisions to hurt you or doesn't care about your future or well-being.

You are in the big leagues now, which means, you have to start being more conscious of who you associate with. Once you have started making genuine profits, it is time to consider doing full background checks on anyone you know on a personal level. Hang out with the person, learn their habits, hobbies, and how they speak about themselves and other people. By person, I mean: you exchange money, products, or services with them; you bring them on board as a business partner; or you bring them into your life as a social partner. It is important to know who you are dealing with. And while I may have an advantage in knowing a little bit more about behavior than the average bear, it does not stop other people from changing their minds, or even being a really good liar or manipulator. Even I get fooled sometimes or thrown off by ignoring my intuition.

When it comes to "building a legacy," you have to think above and beyond your typical 9-5, mid five-figure a year position, and start thinking about what you can build with a person *and* what they can destroy or take from you. Emotions need to take the backseat on this ride. I do my best to believe in people—but I only let them close to me, personally or business-wise, once I know their potential, capabilities, and ultimate intentions. Sometimes you have to pull up your "big-kid" pants and pass up emotional and bodily urges to achieve your goals. Never lose sight of the bigger picture. It also helps to keep the big picture in mind every step of the way. Making better decisions about who you associate with will just be another byproduct of your winning attitude and success. Partner with the best people, and you will have the best— anything you want.

5. Build a lifestyle, not a business.

If you set out to be self-employed, you can do it. If you set out to own a small business, you can do it. If you set out to own a very large franchise, you can do it. Yes, you really can do any and everything you set your mind to, as long as you are willing to become the person it takes to achieve those goals, and perform the necessary action as well. Never forget that you have to follow all of those silly laws of nature, the universe, God, physics... whatever name you choose to associate with a force beyond your control. (You can read about those laws to which I am referring by checking out *Breaking Point Better Edition* or *Breaking Laws of Attraction Better Edition*.)

Think about the bigger picture for a minute. Whatever you are doing for income, do you really want to be doing it? Or would you prefer to make yourself some sort of automated system to create wealth? I don't know about you, but I would much rather build a business around my desire to raise and homeschool my daughter, travel, and have the freedom and money to create as many memorable experiences as I possibly can. For my daughter more than myself. This starts with making the decision to build a way of life. Don't just build a business. Decide who you want to be, where you want to go, and what you want to do, *then* figure out how to make income around it.

6. Don't write a book, unless...

When I first started my publishing company, I started it with the intention of recreating for entrepreneurs the boost I received when I wrote my first book. I immediately saw the benefits of becoming an expert or an authority figure in your field, as I was spending a significant amount of time at networking events when my first book launched. Since being an "author" made my business card and resume look more professional, I decided to build my company strictly for entrepreneurs with the same goal. Later, after making the decision to become a genuine content creator, I changed the focus of my publishing company. Rather than helping entrepreneurs write their first books, I decided we would help anyone launch and market a self-published book with us. Having taken the time to publish multiple manuscripts, audio, video, children's books, etc., I have learned the hassles firsthand of how difficult it can be to find good editors, cover creators, publicists, and people who can genuinely help you market a brand.

The entire reason I started the Legacy Status Systems brand was to build an exclusive network of entrepreneurs who wanted to build global empires, rather than just building a small business. I have been a small business owner (there is nothing wrong with being a small business owner), but I hit a point where I wanted to build something bigger for myself and my daughter – and any other family I could possibly have in the future. Regardless of any of the companies I start or become a part of, intellectual property is of great importance to me now. I do not just want to write books;, I want to make comics, illustrated stories, music, movies, software, and any other medium I can use to spread my voice, ideas, and creativity to the world.

I learned from the great `Stan Lee, after trying to sell his first few comics and getting nowhere fast, he then decided to concentrate on creating more content. It was only a matter of time before he struck gold and Marvel Comics became the household name it is today. While I said I was not going to place a part of Breaking Bad in this book... I think I may have lied, because these few paragraphs resonate with the message I have written here. Be right back:

I don't know if you are aware of this, but there are a lot of new "authors" out there publishing eBooks like business cards, with hopes to increase their web presence and sales base, and to also give themselves the title of "author." I know, I was one of them... but I learned by living – and living taught me, being an author does not make you a true writer. Practice and perfecting your craft can make you a true writer – just like a drummer, or an air conditioning technician, or a painter...

To all of those authors who are writing books to market yourselves, whether you are paying someone to write your 3,000 word eBook or not, you are falling into a trap. With self-publishing being so easy, and droves of entrepreneurs seeing the benefit(s) in having a book to their name, we are essentially creating the next generation of writers. Authors will be faced with a few choices; do they become one hit wonders who publish a document for a more dynamic business card? Will they ever sell any considerable amount of publications in the course of their lifetime, or own a small eBook that just fades into the background? Do they become one of the many authors who never take the time to learn the art of writing, speaking, and communicating... or, do they become the Joe Gores, Stephen King, Robert Crais, and JK Rowling of tomorrow? (I guess you can tell which writers I admired growing up.) Regardless which path is chosen, I would make one solid recommendation; go back to your original manuscript, even if you have only written one, and rewrite it from your heart. Then, get it printed, no matter how big or small it is. Holding my first book in my hand brought forth almost as much emotion as holding Emma for the first time. Taking the time to bring anything of substance into the world can drive us straight to a path to greatness, if we allow it. Sharing ourselves with the people of the planet is exactly why we are here. So share.

I decided, I am a writer. I not only want to continue sharing my stories and perspective, I want my readers to feel, hear, and dive into the passion I pour into my writing. I want to be a household name, with a library of well over 200 books written... and that does not include documentaries, seminars, or the audio presentations I am publishing now. I want to leave a legacy for my family... to make the "Criddle" name mean something. I want to be President of the United States, and show my generation what we can achieve when we pour all of our effort into actually completing something. I want to be responsible for the Global Awakening. I want to leave my mark, so the world will know I cared enough to change myself, to in turn become the right person the planet needed for salvation. – Breaking Bad

Don't write a book unless you are planning to do something with it. When I wrote my first book, I had already planned my first 3. There was always a bigger plan to spread a bigger message. Puffing up your business card with a single book and no desire to "change" anything will just raise a whole lot of questions you may not be willing to answer. Be a content creator. DO SOMETHING with your work—don't just write a book because you think it will make you look better.

7. This is your legacy. Are you doing enough?

About 2 years ago, I created a habit of asking myself, "What should you be doing right now?" It was my way of analyzing my surroundings. Activating the "camera" I have mentioned in the past that follows you throughout the day so you can review the footage at the end of the day. When I ask myself what I should be doing, I can immediately ground myself in the moment, and take a 3rd party perspective of the events taking place in my surroundings. Once I gather a full grasp on my very own actions, I decide whether or not I can be doing something to better myself in any way. If there is something I can be working on that will help build my legacy, I jump on it.

I came up with this little analogy the other day while on a radio show: I said, "If you want to be in a strong relationship, you have to become a strong person first."

So many people have this expectation of someone significant coming into their lives and changing everything for them. Unless you are doing work to change your own future, nothing will change. Now, that does not mean hardships, 20 hour days, and drawing blood, it just means you need to be doing something worthy of building a legacy. If you are not building assets, you are wasting your time.

I used to wonder what the difference between wealth and riches were... then I experienced it. Riches are money. Wealthy is what is left when there is no money... or the byproduct of the money. The "who" and "what" you have become. The "where" you live. The "how" you got to that point. Far too many people focus on making money, when they should focus on giving value to others.

There is an entire truckload of wealth and riches just around the corner, waiting for you. Yes, you. What are you going to do to get it here, and what are you going to do to help it show up on your doorstep? Rather than worrying about making money, you should be thinking about how you can make other people money. How can you enrich other's lives? What, of yourself, can you offer to the world to make them change the entire way they live and experience the world? This is your path to riches.

Steve Jobs did it. Mark Cuban did it. Einstein did it. Edison did it. Whether they were rich or wealthy, you know of their names because of the actions they took and the decisions they made that changed your life, not theirs. The most successful and wealthy people to ever walk this earth created their own careers. So, what are you doing? Are you trying to become a member of society? Or are you trying to become your best self?

If you are focusing on trying to build a career with a title that a million other people share; if you are trying to pass a course with fifty other people in your class, with another class of fifty waiting to walk in after you, while that class is being taken in a thousand schools all across the country, be prepared and stop to look around — because there is your competition right there - waiting for you to fuck up so they can snatch the rug right out from underneath you.

But what about you? Your beautiful self? What about the God that God put within you? What about the drive and passion that you have... the gift that NO ONE on this planet has except you? You know it's in you. You were doing it yesterday. You were complimented on it just last week. This morning, someone told you how great you were at it. And tomorrow, someone will tell you that you should do it for a living. So, why aren't you doing it?

Are you afraid? Is your amygdala causing a little too much fear? Is a little too much cortisol seeping into your bloodstream because of your unfamiliarity with the unknown? Are your friends laughing at you and telling you that it's a stupid idea and you shouldn't do it? Did you try it before for a few months, and you were too damn patient to see it through?

Your way to wealth is to provide value to others. The law of compensation. A little law that I have written about many times which states your will be compensated for the amount of value you bring to the world around you. Money and wealth is the byproduct of your value. A byproduct of your service and contribution. This doesn't mean you have to work your ass off doing something you hate. As a matter of fact, your passion should be the exact opposite. You should not only love what you are doing to become wealthy, but you should want to teach others to do it, pay others to let you do it, and be willing to die happily while you are doing it. Your path to wealth creation exists within you. All you have to do is make the decision to become the "you" that God put you here for. – Understanding the God Theory

8. Do something publicity worthy.

While a lot of spend ample amounts of money on SEO, advertising, and marketing, all of those efforts will eventually die in vain if someone has not taken the time to build a name for themselves. Most small business owners will open up a store, an office, or start a home-based business and follow all of the same step their competition did when setting up shop. The saddest part is, in a lot of cases, their competition has not achieved the milestones they set out to achieve originally. "The blind leading the blind," as the old saying goes.

If you are concentrating on building your name and fulfilling your purpose, some part of what you are doing should make an impact worthy of gaining some publicity and attention. If someone frowns upon your desire to gather some limelight, they may not align with your purpose, and you may seriously need to reconsider having them in your life. Don't do something outstanding or courageous *just* for publicity—it will never work. If you are performing genuine acts of kindness and gratitude, with a true desire to change our planet for the better, your efforts will be rewarded in due time.

9. Get a mentor, or become a mentor.

While some coaches stand firmly behind the idea of finding a mentor, I do not necessarily think one is needed in all cases. There is this saying that goes something like, "Find someone doing what you want to do, follow them, and become successful."

I stand behind the idea that one should realize no one on the planet can do what you can do. Follow your own purpose and passion, then become successful. And while some people are fortunate enough to have access to people who could potentially be mentors, there are others who would rather be the pioneers and explorers of our premature, enlightened future. I do not want to teach others to do what I have done—I want to teach others that they have the power within them to do whatever they want to do. I want to teach others how to build wealth and a free lifestyle based on their dreams, not the dreams of others.

If you do decide you want a mentor, do not ask someone to be your mentor; become a servant and absorb information as you go along. If you do not have access to a mentor, become the badass that God put you here to be.

10. Build something profitable, make it sustainable, and then repeat the process.

I see way too many entrepreneurs fall into one of the very same traps I did, which is jumping from one idea to the next, especially when there is not an immediate payoff from the minimal amount of effort put in. I am not saying some people are not putting in enough effort to see a project through, but for too many times, I have watched someone try to build something for a few weeks, or even a few months, then give up and move onto another project, just to repeat the process.

Of course you have to do what it takes to bring in income and pay the bills, but you have to remember, the bigger your dreams are, the more steps it will take to build a foundation. I purchased the first Legacy Status domain almost 3 years ago, and it is just now getting to the point to where it makes sense. I went through countless sales people, friends who needed jobs, and dozens of NDA's signed; with no real long term success. Persistence and perseverance helped me to bring my dream to life. So many people dream of building their legacy too, but give up long before they ever get close. It doesn't have to be hard or take a lot of work, but it sure will be different. Do yourself a favor, stick to a project until it becomes profitable, make it profitable long term, and THEN move onto the next project.

11. Become a dominant force before you have competition, or take yourself out of the "competition zone."

What can one do to combat competition? Well, that is easy: build a name for yourself. Become an idea, not just a business owner. Go beyond SEO and marketing campaigns. Hustle until you never have to introduce yourself again. If you work to become recognizable in an endless sea of faces, you will automatically stand apart from the crowd. It takes so little effort to be just like everyone else, so put forth as much effort as possible, and completely rid yourself of any competition.

12. Everything unfolds like it should, based on your thoughts and actions. The universe will only bring you what you can handle, have handled, or need to grow to handle later.

If you have not yet read *How Can I*, you should seriously consider it, because Josh's book speaks volumes about this very topic. As many times as Emma has begged me for a pet horse, I still haven't gotten her one, and I cannot imagine doing so in the near future. Why? Because I do not believe she can handle the responsibility yet. She would have to prove herself worthy of taking on such an incredibly daunting task. Perhaps one day, we can start with a fish, or even a puppy, but it would not be very responsible of me to burden her with so much hard work, especially when I know she is not ready for it.

The universe acts the same way. You don't have to reach some farfetched pinnacle of success before fame, fortune, and riches come knocking at your door, but you sure have to start working towards it. While we often hear of people winning the lottery, or coming across great sums of money just to end up broker than they were before, I have learned to find solace in the struggle. If at any moment, I feel even the slightest hint of dissatisfaction with where my life is, or where it is heading, I remember: it is my fault. Rather than becoming angry or upset about my lack of achievement, I come to terms with the reality of the situation, and start making a game plan to tackle the particulars I need to change about myself.

Unfortunately, this simple action is rarely performed by the average person, if ever. So, if you ever find yourself frustrated about the lack of growth or progress in your reality, remember, the universe will only deliver what you can handle. If you want to handle more, then DO more.

13. Always have income.

I think this goes without saying, but you should always have income flowing in. If you are working at a job, do not jump ship just yet. Life becomes a whole lot easier if you can create enough income to replace the 9-to-5 paycheck you are receiving now. Do not put yourself in a situation where you panic about where your next dollar or next meal will come from. This state of survival mode will cause you to make decisions that could very well be detrimental to your future, rather than helpful.

Find simple ways to bring in income if you absolutely refuse, or lack the means to work a "typical" job. There are plenty of freelancing websites online for people with all sorts of skills. Nonprofit organizations are hidden gems for people who could be looking to make some extra income. While there is quite a bit of volunteer work to be had, there are plenty of other perks and opportunities that come along with volunteering your time instead of sitting on your butt. If you don't have a lot of money to invest, start working on building assets through network-marketing or your first pieces of intellectual property. Building leverage is key to building wealth, and passive income.

14. Many of the problems you feel are holding your business at bay were problems long before you had a business. The problem isn't the business – the problem is you.

There are so many of us who want to succeed, but we are not willing to do what it takes to get there. And, what it takes to get there isn't always about tasks or to-do lists. Success comes from the person. As Bob Proctor says, "It is not about making a million dollars. It is about the person you become on the way to making a million dollars." I am paraphrasing of course, but you get the idea.

While so many of us will quickly blame other people in our lives, and not take responsibility for our actions, the ones who succeed are the ones who are willing to own up to their mistakes *and* stop performing the repetitive and sometimes addictive behaviors that have been holding them at bay.

While there are often extenuating circumstances, most of the errors and lack of accomplishments that I have experienced were directly correlated to the actions I did not take. This stems from not becoming the person I needed to be to achieve those goals. Today has been a spectacular day: I have written and edited more than 6,000 words. Could you imagine how much content I would have written if I wrote 6,000 words every day? But I don't. Why?

Because I have not become that person yet. That is only one example—I have a million bajillion things I have to work on myself, but I do realize, I am the one holding back my own success. As I have said before, "Your success is solely dependent upon the second letter in success."

15. Network-Marketing is a good tool to keep in your arsenal.

Everyone is looking for an inexpensive business to invest in, but everyone will talk trash about multi-level marketing. While broke people allow themselves to exist within a paradigm of "pyramid scheme" this and "scam" that, there is a small group of people out there putting forth a tremendous amount of effort into their network marketing companies. This group of people generally consists of 3 different types of network-marketers:

1. The beginners who live on the hype and draw of the company. Because these people take their company's message seriously, they may actually hit it big by proxy, or because an upline decides to hold their hand due to genuine effort or success.

2. The people who signed up to shut someone up, or they don't care enough to ever build the business. You will meet a whole slew of these people in the network-marketing business. And these are usually the people who speak the most negativity towards companies that "never worked."

3. The affluent. The popular. The well connected. These people do great in network-marketing by default because they have already built a following, a brand, a company, etc. There is something they have accomplished which makes network-marketing look easy from the outside.

And do you know why it is easy for them now? Because they probably put forth a whole bunch of effort a long time ago. They deserve respect, regardless of how easy you think you have it.

Regardless of what network-marketing company you get yourself involved in, there are not many other inexpensive, established businesses you can invest in with such a high potential return. Your effort in network-marketing depends solely upon the amount of effort you are willing to put into building your name, not your network-marketing business.

16. Find people who believe in your purpose.

I wanted to take "relationships" a step further and touch more on the types of people you need to surround yourself with. You need people who are on your team. Period. You do not always need a bunch of "yes" men around you either. It is crucial to have members within your entourage who will offer constructive criticism just as much as offering support to help you along your purpose. I do not think people who do not fit in this criteria are not a necessary part of our life; we will always have people in our lives who could care less, people who do not like us, people who do not know we exist... the list goes on and on. The important thing is to be weary of those you allow in your close inner circle. If they are not on your team, they are a waste of your time.

17. Be ready for the explosion of abundance.

I meet so many people who say they want to be rich, but they do not put forth the necessary effort. That is why less than 5% of the population could be considered rich. The other 95% tell themselves lies about why they are not rich in an attempt to make themselves feel better about not doing what it takes. If someone were to come to me and needed a solution to make an extra ten or twenty thousand dollars in the next 12 months, there would be thousands, if not millions of options available to us. If someone were to come to me and needed a solution to make an extra million dollars in the next 12 months, suddenly we are faced with much fewer options that will require an approach beyond the subtleties of a five figure a year income. Unless this person already possessed the knowledge to make this kind of income, meaning, they had done it before.

The truth is, if you are going to build an empire, you have to be willing to build the foundation of an empire. When I wrote my first book, I instantly learned the power of having my first asset. Then came a second, and a third. Then I started a publishing company so I could not only help other writers publish their work, but I would also get my hands on more assets. A foundation is built stone by stone, brick by brick. There are so many pieces to the "get rich" puzzle, and one of those pieces is your first asset. Then the next and the next. You have to continue to build assets, or build a foundation whether you are in real estate, business investments, stocks, or intellectual property. There are not many "jobs" you can do that will land you in any sort of "rich" category.

You need leverage. Leverage comes from taking what you have and doing as much as you can with it. The more you have, the more you can do with it. This is why you constantly need to be creating content, building a name for yourself, building an entourage of good people, and working towards the big picture. Wealth is what you are left with when the money is gone, and no one can take wealth away from you. Wealth brings you abundance, and when the world learns who you are, you need to be ready for them. If you have nothing for them to buy, you will miss a crucial piece to the "get rich" puzzle.

18. "Don't play football if you are not willing to tackle someone." – Greg Doss

When I was going through my custody battle, a buddy of mine told me the quote above. Not only was he a radio host and a constitutional law expert, he was also a little league football coach. On the first day of practice, he would lay down his rules and expectations he had for and of his players. One of those expectations was tackling. Not just to be tackled, but to get tackled.

I think a lot of us business owners are willing to get tackled; some are even willing to get back up. Society teaches us to persevere, but no one has really taught us to attack. Why build a company with a strong defensive plan and exit strategy when you can build a company that will completely blow your competition out of the water? Instead of trying to improve upon the things your competition is doing, why don't you instead find out what your competition is not doing, or would never think of doing?

19. Are you really an entrepreneur? Or do you just own a job?

Entrepreneur is such a fun word, and often misused too. While the average "job" owner will call themselves an entrepreneur, I like to think of its true meaning as being a little closer to the dictionary definition; an entrepreneur manages multiple projects while making above-average risks. I would also like to throw in there, an entrepreneur typically understand the importance of an asset, and works towards building assets, rather than bringing in immediate income.

A plumber is not an entrepreneur; the owner of a plumbing company with many contractors, assets, equipment, and cash flow is an entrepreneur. A doctor is not an entrepreneur; the guy who spent zero time in medical school and owns the hospital where the doctor practices medicine is an entrepreneur. A young lady who quits her job to become a maid is not an entrepreneur. Sadly, she needs people making money for her before she can consider herself an entrepreneur.

Remember, there is nothing wrong with being a small business or job owner, just make sure you know what an entrepreneur is before you start calling yourself one.

"The average job, which accounts for a majority of the populous, has a starting point where the result is already placed in front of the employee. They are then taught how to mimic the result. This behavior then produces thoughts in the subconscious mind, which produce feelings about the thought. These feelings drive the person into action. These actions cycle back to the original result. This behavior is continually repeated until the mind is forced to revert back to the original cycle, rather than finding innovative solutions to create a better result, the mind is motivated to repeat the same behavior.

When people have the ability to choose or create certain results for themselves, they are forced to come up with an idea. The idea then produces thoughts, which create feelings of emotion about the idea. *Those feelings then drive them into action. These actions produce their very own result, based upon their original creative idea. Rather than being told to mimic the result from the beginning, this cycle reverts back to the creation of more ideas, be it innovation, or entirely new paths to explore.*" – Trainer to Trillionaire

20. The best sales person does not have to sell anything.

I remember when I first got into network-marketing. I do not mean to talk about it so much, but it was kind of my gateway drug into assets, wealth, vision boards, and manifestation. Network-marketing helped me believe I really could become rich and afford all of the subtleties of life only a select few enjoy. Once I started thinking big, I never looked back.

I realized, I could talk anyone into network-marketing, regardless of what company I was involved with. But it never had to do with the company, it had to do with the beliefs the people had in me. Were it not for my desire to educate myself, make real changes in my community, and actively take steps to become a better human being, I would not be the person I am today. And the person I am today doesn't have to sell anything. I rarely even have to show up anymore. People know that when my name or my brands are involved, value comes along without question. I have worked diligently to construct a brand name within myself, and because of that hard work, I no longer have to sell anything.

21. Life will always happen. Don't let it get in the way.

You are not just waking up and giving it your all so you can be the absolute best— you are giving it your all so you can be the absolute best on even your worst day. Some people believe I stay positive *all* the time. They think I never have bad days or upset feelings. This is not true. I do have bad days. I too live with daily frustrating situations. But I also realize, there is a time to be frustrated. Just as there is a time to be angry, impatient, or sad. Ignoring these feelings and emotions does nothing for us, except cause our body to operate in a deficit or a mindset of resistance—it is nearly impossible to "not think" about something by ignoring it. During those times of frustration, embrace your emotions, confront the problem, and find the quickest solution necessary to regain peace of mind.

Allow yourself to have a minute, an hour, or even a day to "feel bad," and remember, it is just a feeling. Saying "I am" only causes you to identify with a problem, which in turn causes the pain or emotion you are feeling to become a permanent part of your being. Saying "I feel" allows your body and mind to still feel empowered, even when life is doing something you might not particularly like. Remember: pain is necessary, but suffering is optional. We suffer when we put ourselves in a deficit or in a mindset of resistance. Let life happen, and do your best to stay in control. It will be much easier to dust yourself off once

you realize this simple fact: Life really does
go on.

22. If you are not prepared to fail, you are not prepared to succeed.

In principle number 19, I mentioned a
behavior cycle I came up with for *Trainer to
Trillionaire*. While there are a lot of us who
want to succeed in creating a gigantic
business, we must prepare ourselves for
one of the most crucial elements of success.
That element, is failure.

While you have been taught your entire
life to shy away from making mistakes,
fearing the reprisal of an upset teacher,
disappointed boss, or misunderstanding
spouse, mistakes absolutely must be made
in order to reach your goals. Why? Because
there is absolutely no way anyone will ever
reach their long term goals the first time
out. Failing allows us to critique the
process, create a better value proposition
for our product or service, or move onto a

different path entirely. I am not an advocate of giving up on your goals, however, I am an advocate of continually working towards a goal until you are absolutely certain it will not work, then moving on.

Michael Jordan attributes all of the accomplishments he achieved in his lifetime of playing basketball to the sheer volume of failures he experienced. If he had given up on himself after any one single failure, the sport of basketball may be played completely different today. At your typical job these days, a failure can land you a reprimand or even a spot in the unemployment line. In the life of the entrepreneur, you really only have to be "right" once in order to experience the successes you desire.

23. Don't try to do it all on your own— whenever possible, delegate a task.

Being a trainer for quite some time, I met a lot of people who only wanted to work on their strengths. Men who neglected their legs for a more powerful chest would naturally gravitate towards the bench press as I would lead them to the leg press. Women with powerful glutes and hamstrings would head over to the leg press as I would walk them to the bench press to strengthen their upper body. While I spent many years turning "Averages Joes" into competitive athletes by focusing on their weaknesses, the exact opposite holds true when you are dealing with a startup business.

Sadly, I have wasted a great deal of time as an entrepreneur, focusing too much of my time on my weaknesses rather than focusing on my strengths. While I spent a great deal of my life carrying so much pride in my ability to multitask and learn new skills, I have found now, success comes from concentrating on what I am good at, (and hopefully, what you are good at makes money) and paying someone else to do the tasks I don't have time to get to. When I get an idea for a new cd, I gather whatever audio I need to gather, and send it to the studio. When I finish a manuscript, I pass it off to an editor. A year ago I would have purchased an in-home audio studio to learn the art of manipulating sound on my own. As for my manuscripts, I would probably be on the 28th edit of my 3rd book—instead of working on books 14 through 20. Both tasks would have taken a considerable amount of time and energy; effort I could have been applying towards the creation of more content, instead of executing menial tasks I don't have the education to perform.

24. Be open to any opportunity.

There is more than one way to tie a shoe, skin a cat, and make passive income. I spoke earlier about entrepreneurs who give up on opportunities before they have time to seed, sprout, and grow; that being said, I may have forgotten to mention how good it could be for you to take on a second, third, or even tenth venture.

"Don't put all of your eggs in one basket." Meaning, there is nothing wrong with working towards multiple streams of income at once. Don't stretch yourself so thin that you are losing sleep, sanity, or money, but don't pass up on an opportunity just because it seems like "work." Sometimes, borrowing a little time and energy from one project could very well make giant waves in another. Follow your gut, and if you feel inspired to start on a new opportunity, go for it.

25. Yes, you should appreciate what you have, but you MUST be hungry for more. Always.

Being grateful plays a major role in starting anything successful. Possessing the ability to give, receive, try, and fail, blah, blah, blah—this is a skill that is not to be taken lightly. Gratitude takes practice, just as mindfulness and awareness do. Far too many of us hold grudges against the world because, "it just isn't fair." Why must everything always be so difficult? We can we not just have the things we want?

I never did understand it when someone told me, "You won't have your dream car until you love and appreciate the car you have." While I can see their point about appreciation, I hardly loved my car. And while I was indeed grateful for having a vehicle to safely transport my daughter and me from point A to point B, I could still be hungry for something better.

We lie to ourselves way too often, telling ourselves we are okay with our small apartment, subpar vehicle, or even our unfulfilling relationships. But we tell ourselves this lie so we can feel better about not doing what it takes to have something better. When the body gets hungry, the mind searches for food—this is the same principle that should be applied to your wealth, brand, and any businesses you have, each and every day. Be grateful for everything you have, but stay hungry. The hunger will keep you on the search for more.

My uncle always told me, "The only thing that happens when you retire, is you die."

Sadly, after he retired, he passed on. Why? Because "the search" is what keeps the human alive. Our will to live comes from our desire to grow, and the opposite of growth, is death. If you want to keep growing, you have to keep eating, so stay hungry.

26. Make reading, relaxation, and exercise a priority, every day.

I am not going to talk about exercise. I have talked about it enough in many of my books. I will say however, make time for the gym. Getting the blood flowing, the heart pumping, and the muscles aching are just as good for business as they are for the heart and brain. Why? Stress and anger elimination, weight loss, increased confidence, increased endorphins and "happy" hormones, boost in brain computing power, sharper memory, better sleep... do I really need to keep going?

The library is free—did you know that? Oh yeah? Then why does less than 3% of the country's population have a library card? Because our education system destroyed what books represent. There hits a point in just about every child's life where they stop looking at a trip to the library as a fun adventure, and start looking at it as a useless chore; just a place to study or kill time on the computer. There are over 130 million books in circulation today, and all of them are waiting to captivate your imagination, teach you how to build a homemade helicopter, or yes, even build a lucrative, multimillion dollar business. But the trick is, you have to read them. Turn off your TV, close out Facebook, and get lost in a real book.

And while you are doing all of that, don't forget to "take a chill pill" (as Emma would say). Have you ever floated a river? It is seriously one of the most fun and relaxing experiences you will ever have. Do you know how to do it? Take a bunch of floats and a bunch of friends to a river, sit down in the floats, and have the time of your life. This steady flow of the water can perfectly describe life's steady flow of abundance. At some point in your life, someone told you that "hard work" was the only way to achieve your goals. Well, since that hasn't worked, try my advice for a little while. Relax. Stop resisting, and let the current carry you to your destiny.

27. Be as open and transparent as possible.

So many of us are afraid of our competition, but we don't realize, competition is almost non-existent once we make the choice to create something. No one can steal an original idea and you cannot accuse someone of stealing an idea if you decide to do nothing with it. In the early days of Legacy Status Systems, I spent more time having potential sales people read and sign non-disclosure agreements than I ever did training them. I was so worried about someone stealing our "trade secrets," I never took the time to properly motivate my team or give any direction to my contractors. It was only after I "let go" of this mistrust that my business started moving anywhere.

Now, rather than being so secretive, we happily let new contractors, artists, and "Average Joes" take a look at our business model and patented interface system. One of the first tasks my development team performs when bringing a new designer on board is participating in an open forum discussion of where we are, where we want to be, and how we can grow further as a team. There are no trade secrets anymore, and there are even customers we cannot handle either. So what do we do? We share. We share information, we pass on customers, and we make recommendations based on the betterment of everyone involved, not just the company.

Writing books about my life has helped me to become more open and transparent as well. Vulnerability gives you a strength money cannot buy: freedom.

28. You are your only competition—if you make your goals big enough.

I mentioned earlier:

If someone were to come to me and needed a solution to make an extra ten or twenty thousand dollars in the next 12 months, there would be thousands, if not millions of options available to us. If someone were to come to me and needed a solution to make an extra million dollars in the next 12 months, suddenly we are faced with much fewer options that will require an approach beyond the subtleties of a five figure a year income

.For just a moment, imagine society as a pyramid. At the bottom of the pyramid is 99.9% of the population, fighting to achieve average goals and milestones. The further you travel up the top of the pyramid, the lonelier your life becomes. Why? Because there isn't as much competition at the top. There aren't as many people trying to make a billion dollars as there are people trying to make an extra twenty. Action and perseverance will help you achieve your goals, but I must admit, it is rather fun having goals so large that no one can get in my way—except myself of course.

29. Position yourself wisely. There is nothing worse than becoming great at something useless.

John D. Rockefeller had his entire fortune in marine shipping when he caught a glimpse of a train just outside his office window. Even though he had seen the train stopped at the station many times, this particular instance filled his mind and body with a paradigm shift and a whole new manner in which to construct his business. Almost overnight, he pulled all of his money out of shipping and invested everything in the railway system. I know I am skipping a lot of details, but know that this move eventually led to the boom of the railway industry, the automotive industry, the oil industry, and practically every single facet of life we enjoy today.

Mr. Rockefeller positioned himself wisely. In one single glimpse, he saw a whole new way to ship merchandise and travel. Whale oil was being used to keep our homes lit, and boats just couldn't get cargo across the US fast enough, nor could a boat drive right into the center of the country to deliver goods either. Steve Jobs knew that people wanted to "carry 1,000 songs in their pocket," and Mark Zuckerberg knew people wanted to be "present" on the internet.

In *The Valuation Evaluation*, I discuss the never-ending amount of "great" ideas I came across in the early stages of owning Legacy Status Investments. That said, a lot of the business plans I looked at were a result of bad positioning. There are way too many entrepreneurs focused on "improvement" when we should be focusing on "innovation." We are explorers, not babysitters and caretakers. A good entrepreneur positions himself where the marketplace is making money; a great entrepreneur creates a new marketplace.

30. Get paid for what you do. Discounts are for people who do not know their worth. Get paid just for being yourself.

Do not offer discounts. Do not devalue yourself. Offering something for free is just silly. If you are offering free products or services to not only fulfill the laws of the universe, but also bring more attention and value to your business, that is one thing... To give someone a price for the position you have allowed yourself to get paid for, and then offer discounts, or devalue yourself, can show a lack of confidence in your ability to lead or direct. Some will say, "Well, I will only discount in the beginning..."

No you won't. You will find yourself in a trap of forever offering discounts to friends, family, associates, etc. Set a price and stick with it. You are worth it. – Trainer to Trillionaire

On a daily basis, I take at least a half hour to myself for affirmations and breathing exercises. This does not coincide with my prayer or meditation because I do believe these are very separate practices.

That being said, I do have quite a few mantras that have stuck with me, regardless of how much I feel I've evolved in my life. One of those mantra is: I get paid just for being me.

In my early stages of being a trainer, being a speaker, and even being an author, I would often have to step outside of myself and realize that I AM the reason people respond to me – not my title or my position. When I first came back to Dallas and applied for a position at the big box gym I worked out of, I was actually afraid of being a small fish in a very big pond. I thought my title of "Personal Trainer" increased my value and worth as a person. But I soon realized, I brought value and worth to the industry.

You shouldn't be focused on building a job or a business; you should focus on building yourself. It doesn't matter if you want better friends, better pay, better opportunities, or a better relationship, building your "self" is the only answer.

In closing...

This list will definitely grow. Had I written this manuscript a year ago, it probably would have only consisted of 5 to 8 principles. Not to mention, all of the grammar and syntax errors you would have found throughout the book. I enjoy sharing content and ideas with you. And I really only do it to show others that they can do it to.

You picked up this book, whether a big version of it, or a small one, because you are interested in building a legacy. Something inside you is screaming for you to wake up and stop living an average, incomplete, and unfulfilled life. You are the only thing that has ever held you back. So, if you are building a global empire, and things get tough, remember: they are supposed to be. Once you made the decision to stop following the crowd, you invited all of those hardships into your life. If building something bigger than yourself was easy, there would just be "the way," and everyone would do it. But there isn't just one way. And if you are reading any of my books, it is because you know you need as much help as you can get. Build yourself a kick ass business, and don't blow your head off along the way.